InfoTrac® College Edition
Student Activities Workbook for
PUBLIC SPEAKING 2.0

Victoria Linn Howitt
Grossmont College

THOMSON

WADSWORTH

Australia • Canada • Mexico • Singapore • Spain • United Kingdom • United States

Printed in the United States of America
  2 3 4 5 6 7 07 06 05

Printer: Globus Printing

ISBN 0-534-53099-0

For more information about our products, contact us at:
Thomson Learning Academic Resource Center
1-800-423-0563

For permission to use material from this text, contact us by:
Phone: 1-800-730-2214
Fax: 1-800-731-2215
Web: http://www.thomsonrights.com

Wadsworth/Thomson Learning
10 Davis Drive
Belmont, CA 94002-3098
USA

Asia
Thomson Learning
5 Shenton Way #01-01
UIC Building
Singapore 068808

Australia/New Zealand
Thomson Learning
102 Dodds Street
Southbank, Victoria 3006
Australia

Canada
Nelson
1120 Birchmount Road
Toronto, Ontario M1K 5G4
Canada

Europe/Middle East/South Africa
Thomson Learning
High Holborn House
50/51 Bedford Row
London WC1R 4LR
United Kingdom

Latin America
Thomson Learning
Seneca, 53
Colonia Polanco
11560 Mexico D.F.
Mexico

Spain/Portugal
Paraninfo
Calle/Magallanes, 25
28015 Madrid
Spain

Contents

INTRODUCTION AND ORIENTATION TO
InfoTrac College Edition Communication Activities Workbook

In the last few years, many communication students have discovered that electronic sources, such as the Internet, hold an amazingly rich fund of information that can be used when creating speeches. The convenience of being able to find and select the supporting information for a speech topic without leaving the comforts of home is highly appealing to many students. However, the complexity and vastness of cyberspace can be overwhelming, intimidating, and even time-wasting, especially for those who are new to electronic searches. You are about to be introduced, through this workbook, to a manageable electronic virtual library that will not only allow you, from your first visits to **InfoTrac,** to efficiently research speech topics, but also provide you with resources for learning more about human communication.

Types of InfoTrac Articles Used for Workbook Activities

The activities in this workbook rely on three different uses of the materials that can be acquired through **InfoTrac**. The first application of materials is the one that has already been mentioned, providing supporting material for classroom speeches. **InfoTrac** indexes and can supply full-length articles from hundreds of periodicals, covering a wide variety of subjects. In several chapters of the workbook, most notably Chapter 6 on Researching Your Speech in the Information Age, you will be guided through the process of researching a speech topic of your choice using **InfoTrac**. Once you become familiar with **InfoTrac**, it can become your automatic source for locating supporting information for speeches. Using articles from **InfoTrac** has an advantage over some materials located in a general web search because you can have confidence in the authorship and validity of the already published articles found through **InfoTrac**.

The second function of the materials from **InfoTrac** in workbook activities is to supply transcripts of speeches that can serve as models for speech assignments or texts for analysis. Your public speaking textbook provides many examples from speeches and may even include a limited number of full-length speeches. The speeches you work with in the workbook (see Chapters 7, 10, 15, 16 for examples) will complement what you find in your text and also introduce you to the kinds of speeches people in the business and professional worlds are making to real-world audiences.

The final use of **InfoTrac** materials are articles that give you more information about many topics found in your communication textbooks related to speech preparation and presentation. This category includes social scientific research articles that present results of communication studies on various topics and also articles written by people who focus on communication as part of their jobs, telling about their observations and how they have solved communication challenges.

Suggestions for Use of Activity Questions and Responses

Students may use a number of different styles or formats when writing responses to the workbook activity prompts and questions. The choice of response depends on the class goal or use of the activity. The entire set of exercises may be completed individually by the student for the purpose of enriching the student's knowledge and understanding about communication. With this approach, the instructor may, or may not, see or hear the individual answers. If the work is to be graded, it is likely that the student would be expected to write complete, rather formal answers. If, instead, the workbook functions more as a journal of human communication exploration, then the student would be free to use a more individual and personal style of response, one that serves primarily to guide the student's thinking about the topic. Check with your instructor before completing the work.

Many of the activities could be used as the basis for class reports or preparation for class discussion. In such cases, while reading, the students will look for information to share with others and will then write notes to prompt them in their oral reports or in class discussion. One of the best ways to use activities that lend themselves to discovery or evaluation is to work in small groups together on the activity and report to the larger class.

Still other activities may form an integral part of the preparation of speeches that students will actually present in the classroom. Here the responses need to be in a form that is useful to the student and that, at the same time, can show the instructor that the student is making progress on the interim steps of speech preparation.

Suggestions for Getting Started in InfoTrac

Using the Quick Start Guide and your passcode, follow the process given to enter **InfoTrac**. Before you start your first search, while still in EasySearch, click "Easy Search Help." Print a copy of these instructions and read them before you proceed. (Keep the copy in a convenient place where you can refer to it as needed). Next, click on the PowerTrac icon. Bring up and copy the instructions for PowerTrac by clicking on "PowerTrac Help." You may then want to return to EasySearch and spend some time just trying out different search terms to become more familiar with what happens on the screen as a search is conducted. This will give you enough background to find the articles you need for the first five chapters of the workbook. You will notice that for each article used in an activity, you are given a suggested search term to use to locate that article. In Chapter 5, Selecting a Topic and Purpose, and Chapter 6, Researching Your Speech in the Information Age, you will be led through the steps necessary to do independent searches for topics of your choice.

It is very easy to get impatient with the amount of time it takes for an article or search results to come up on the screen. The tendency is to click the button again to remind the machine you're waiting. This can be counter productive and interrupt the movement you are so anxious to see. Instead, pay attention to the information at the bottom of the screen that will tell you when the task is complete and you can enter another command.

CHAPTER 1: Introduction to Public Speaking

Activity 1.1: Importance of Public Speaking for Careers and Jobs

Summary of Activity: You will use articles from **InfoTrac** to explore the role of public speaking skills in the workplace.

1. Locate and read **one** of the following three articles that include information about the need for communication/public speaking skills in the workplace: **"The Importance of Communication and Public-Speaking Skills" by Leo F. Parvis** (*hint: use "public speaking skills" as your search term*), "**Are You a 'Great Communicator'?" by Peter Varhol**, or **"Don't Doubt Your Speaking Potential" by Roger Allan,** (*hint: use "career skills" as your search term*). At this point you may skim the sections of the articles that focus on speaking tips.

2. These articles represent fields (health care and engineering) that may not be automatically associated with giving public speeches. Compare what you have read here with the career that you hope to pursue.

Write down examples of public speaking you might be expected to do in your chosen career.

_____

_____

_____

3. Search **InfoTrac** to determine the role of public speaking in your chosen career. You will probably want to search by the name of the career field (e.g. nursing, industrial engineering, dentistry). Report on the information you find.

_____

_____

_____

_____

Activity 1.2: Public Speaking and Culture

Summary of Activity: You will locate and read an article from **InfoTrac** that gives advice to business people regarding ways to best plan international meetings.

1. Locate and read the following article: "**Bridging the Culture Gap: Sensitivity to Attendees' Languages and Learning Styles Enhances the Meeting Experience**" by Sally J. Walton (*hint: use search term "Intercultural Communication" as a keyword in **PowerTrac***).

2. What has Walton suggested about formality in a meeting to address the learning styles of your audience that you could adapt into your in-class presentations?

_____

3. While you may not find yourself responsible for planning an international meeting in the near future, what are two suggestions (additional to the one you mentioned in question 2) that you can incorporate into your future in-class presentations?

_____

_____

_____

4. Consider your own cultural background in relation to public speaking. Name subject areas you might speak about in this class that reflect your personal background that probably differ from the background of at least some of the students in your classroom audience. The subject areas may be related to beliefs, values, and/or attitudes.

_____

_____

5. Why is it important to consider culture when beginning to learn about public speaking?

_____

Activity 1.3: The History and Tradition of Public Speaking in Education

Summary of Activity: The article from **InfoTrac College Edition** that is the basis for this activity provides an opportunity to learn more about the long history of public speaking as taught and practiced by students since the time of classical Greece and Rome. The history of extra-curricular speaking, such as competitive debate and forensics, is intertwined with the history and tradition of classroom public speaking.

1. Locate and read the following article: **"Foreword: A Long and Proud Tradition" by Ronald F. Reid** (*hint: use the search term "public speaking and history" in PowerTrac*).

2. Notice that in your public speaking text, several reasons or motives for studying public speaking are given. These reasons include both benefits for the society and for the speaker. Compare the motives for studying public speaking in Greek and Roman times with the present day rationales for learning about public speaking. How are the motives different? How are they alike?

_____

_____

_____

3. The article covers a long history of public speaking in education of over 2,000 years. Although the forms and relative importance of classroom and extracurricular speaking have varied, public speaking instruction and practice have continued to be a part of what the Western World has considered necessary for a "complete" education. Give three reasons why public speaking as an academic subject has endured.

_____

_____

_____

_____

CHAPTER 2: Ethics and Public Speaking

Activity 2.1: Analyzing Political Speaking for Exaggeration and Dishonesty

Summary of Activity: In order to reflect on the ethics of exaggeration and dishonesty in public statements, you will use an article from **InfoTrac** focusing on how U.S. politicians have deviated from the truth.

1. Locate and make a copy of **"Al Gore and the Fib Factor: Cleaning Up His Image in Politics Where Truth-telling is Never as Simple as It Sounds" by Jonathan Alter** (*hint: use the search term "politics and truth"*).

2. Read through the article and either highlight or underline all examples of exaggeration or deception by political speakers you find. Count and write down the number of examples you located.

_____

3. Based on the article, what are some reasons political figures exaggerate or present untrue information?

_____

_____

_____

4. Using what you have read in your text or covered in your public speaking class, evaluate the "lies" named in the article to determine if they are unethical or not. Make notes below about the ethical violations you see in the article and then discuss your judgments with others in your class.

_____

_____

_____

5. What is the audience response when speakers (either political speakers or classroom speakers) repeatedly distort the truth?

_____

_____

Activity 2.2: Personal Attacks and Ethics

Summary of Activity: You will locate and read two articles about verbal insults and attacks on groups by a public speaker. You will then apply your insights to speaking in the classroom.

1. Locate, print and read "**Tuning Out Dr. Laura: Do the Fierce Protests Against Her New TV Talk Show Violate the Shock Doc's First Amendment Rights?**" **by David France** and "**Dr. Laura Apologizes to Gays and Lesbians**" (*hint: use "Dr. Laura" as your search term*).

2. In the articles, underline or highlight the examples of personal attacks or insults Dr. Laura has directed toward specific groups.

3. Based on your public speaking text or course content, are her remarks illegal (   ), unethical (   ), both (   ), neither (   )?

Give reasons for your choice.

_____

_____

_____

4. Name at least three speech topic areas that speakers might use for classroom speeches where the speakers need to monitor their language choices to insure the ethical practice of sensitivity and civility toward others.

_____

_____

_____

Activity 2.3: Plagiarism From the World Wide Web

Summary of Activity: You will locate and read an article that examines plagiarism by students using the World Wide Web. You will then consider the implications.

1. Locate, copy and read **"Truth or Consequences" by David Oliver Relin** (*hint: use search term "cheating"*).

2. Define "plagiarism."

_____

3. Make a list of reasons students take speeches or original speech materials that someone else has created and present them as their own.

_____

_____

_____

4. According to the article, what arguments are given to explain why students plagiarize from the Web?

_____

_____

_____

5. How are these arguments flawed?

_____

_____

_____

6. If you wanted to persuade someone not to plagiarize, what information from the article is most effective to support your case?

_____

CHAPTER 3: Managing Speech Apprehension

Activity 3.1: Coping with Public Speaking Anxiety in Real World Settings

Summary: You will read three articles from **InfoTrac** that focus on advice for managing nervousness and apprehension related to speaking in front of groups in non-classroom situations. You will then respond to the advice given by the writers.

1. Locate and read the following articles: **"Taming the Beast Within: 6 Coaches Share Their Secrets for Conquering Speaking Anxiety" by Mark Merritt, "Patterns of Psychological State Anxiety in Public Speaking as a Function of Anxiety Sensitivity" by Ralph R. Behnke and Chris R. Sawyer** (*hint: try search term "speaking anxiety"*), and **"Overcome Your Fear of Speaking and Express Yourself" by Jeffrey Gitomer** (*hint: use "speaking fear" as your search term*).

2. According to the articles, why do people experience speech apprehension?

_____

_____

3. From each of the articles pick out and write down **three ideas or pieces of information** that you found most helpful or worthwhile.

"Taming the Beast Within"

A._____

B._____

C._____

"Patterns of Psychological State Anxiety"

A._____

B._____

C._____

"Overcome Your Fear"

A. _____

B. _____

C. _____

4. Now record suggestions from any of the articles with which you disagree or find questionable.

_____

_____

_____

_____

_____

_____

_____

Activity 3.2: Treatment of Severe Communication Apprehension

Summary of Activity: After reading about social anxiety disorder, a condition so disabling that it interferes with individuals' abilities to work or maintain interpersonal relationships; you will be asked to respond to what you have read in the article.

1. Locate and read the following article using **InfoTrac: "Social Anxiety Disorder: How to Help" by H. Michael Zal** (*hint: use "social anxiety disorder" as a keyword search term*).

2. Compare your personal symptoms of communication anxiety to the symptoms the article describes.

_____

_____

_____

3. List any of the strategies under the category of "behavior therapy" and "cognitive-behavior therapy" that you think you would find helpful in reducing nervousness about public speaking.

_____

_____

_____

_____

4. What personal lesson can you take away from this article?

_____

_____

_____

_____

Activity 3.3: Using Visualization to Increase Performance Confidence

Summary of Activity: The **InfoTrac** article you will use for this activity describes the use of mental imaging or visualization to prepare athletes for competition. Similar techniques can be used effectively for preparing to give a speech. In this activity you are asked to apply the advice for athletes and coaches to the speaking situation.

1. Locate the articles **"Visualization Can Be Tool for Positive Changes" by Jeff Herring** (*hint: use the keyword search term "visualization"*) and "**How an Optimistic Outlook Can Give You an Edge" by Robert D. Ramsey** (*hint: use the subject search term "optimism" and click on periodicals*).

2. Go through the guidelines given in the articles and list the top five suggestions you think you can use to improve your own effectiveness in a public speaking situation.

1. _____

2. _____

3. _____

4. _____

5. _____

3. Make a tentative list of the parts of the speech presentation you will visualize (e.g. walking to the front of the room, looking at the faces of the audience, saying the first words of introduction, etc.).

_____

_____

_____

_____

4. Then, in a situation conducive to relaxation and concentration, try the process of visualizing yourself successfully presenting your speech, taking the time to go through each part of the presentation you have identified above. Alternatively, your instructor may want to lead the entire class in a visualization exercise.

5. Briefly write your reaction to the visualization experience.

_____

_____

_____

_____

Chapter 4: Listening

Activity 4.1: Poor Listening Concerns, Practices and Remedies

Summary of Activity: You will use two articles located through **InfoTrac** to increase your knowledge about the general lack of effective listening skills, why people are poor listeners and possible guidelines for changing listening habits. In addition, you will be able to evaluate your own listening skills.

1. Locate, print and read the following articles: "**Listening: Hear Today, Probably Gone Tomorrow" by Eileen Brill Wagner**, (*hint: search for this article using the search term "listening"*) and "**Communication Survival Skills for Managers" by Stephen J. Romano**. (*hint: use the search term "communication and skills"*).

2. List the explanations given in the article **"Listening: Hear Today, Probably Gone Tomorrow"** for why people are poor listeners.

_____

_____

_____

_____

3. Evaluate the explanations in #2 and mark each one as either "agree," "disagree," "don't know."

4. In the article, "**Listening: Hear Today**," locate the list of "Poor Listening Habits." On your copy of the article, note how frequently you use each ineffective behavior by using the terms: "never," "occasionally," "frequently," "almost always."

Name the three poor listening behaviors you use the most often.

_____

_____

_____

5. Now, go near the end of the article, **"Communication Survival Skills for Managers"** to "Understanding the Employee" and "Using Active Listening Skills." Use the same terms for how often each of these statements is true for you to mark each statement: "never," "occasionally," "frequently," "almost always."

How many did you mark "almost always"? _____

6. Overall how would you evaluate yourself as a listener?

_____

7. Check back to both articles for suggestions on how to improve listening. From either article or both, select three recommendations you will work on to improve your listening skills.

_____

_____

_____

Activity 4.2: Background on Listening

Summary of Activity: In this activity, you will be introduced to some of the theory and research about listening from three **InfoTrac** articles

1. Locate the following three articles: **"Learning to Listen" by James R. Davis and Adelaide B. Davis**; **"Just Listening" by Sandra Hagevik** (*hint: use "listening" as the search term.*); and **"Men Use Only One Side of Brain When Listening; Women Use Both"** (*hint: use "listening and brain" as the search term*).

2. From the article **"Learning to Listen,"** identify the **three listening processes** the brain carries out.

_____

_____

3. Now refer to the article, **"Men Use Only One Side of Brain When Listening: Women Use Both."**

Briefly explain the technique the researchers used to learn more about the brain during the information-processing phase of listening.

_____

_____

_____

_____

What were the results of the investigation?

_____

_____

_____

4. Go next to the article, **"Just Listening."** On approximately the second page of the article, read the section on "The Kinds of Listening." At the top of the next page, list examples of the situations under which you are most apt to use each kind of listening.

When do you use Empathic Listening?

_____

_____

When do you use Hearing Words?

_____

_____

When do you use Listening in Spurts?

_____

_____

Activity 4.3: Improving the Memory Element of Listening

Summary of Activity: Memory may be the part of listening that requires the most deliberate active involvement by the listener. In the activity, you will be introduced to a number of memory strategies that you can learn to incorporate in your listening.

For this activity you will use the **InfoTrac** article **"Learning to Listen" by James R. Davis and Adelaide B. Davis** *(hint: use the search term "listening")*. If you did **Activity 4.2**: Background on Listening, you should already have the article. If not, locate and print the article. Focus on the section of the article on approximately page 3 titled "MEMORY."

1. Explain why "remembering" is considered a part of listening.

_____

_____

_____

_____

2. Read about the five memory techniques discussed in the article: **rehearsal, encoding, imagery, place method, and meaning making**. Memorize the names of the five techniques by using one of the strategies.

What strategy did you use? What specifically did you do?

_____

_____

_____

_____

3. Pick out one of the classroom speeches of a fellow classmate in the next sequence of speeches in your public speaking class. Have as your goal that you will remember twenty-four hours after the speech 10 pieces of information from the speech without taking notes. Use any or all of the memory techniques.

On the day following the speech, list the specific information you remember.

_____

_____

_____

_____

_____

_____

_____

_____

_____

4. Which memory strategy or strategies worked best for you?

_____

Activity 4.4: Note-taking Using Graphic Organizers

Summary: You will locate and read a research article about a method of making notes when listening or reading that promotes retention of the information better than note-taking in outline form. This article will provide the springboard to think about what note-taking techniques are most helpful to you when listening to public speakers.

1. Locate **"Getting Students 'Partially' Involved in Note-Taking Using Graphic Organizers" by Andrew D. Katayama and Daniel H. Robinson** (*hint: try the search term "note-taking"*). NOTE: For this activity, you do not need to read the entire article. The relevant information is in the **first three pages** (when the article is printed out). You may stop reading three paragraphs above "FIGURE 3."

2. What are the most important differences between taking notes using an outline format and taking notes using a graphic organizer?

_____

_____

_____

_____

3. What is the connection between remembering information and using a graphic organizer to take notes?

_____

_____

_____

4. When you take notes on oral lectures, what method or technique do you usually use?

_____

_____

5. What have you discovered about your own style of note-taking that promotes retention of what you see and hear when listening to a speech or lecture?

_____

_____

_____

_____

6. Experiment with using spatial elements in your note-taking (such as graphic organizers, knowledge maps, or concepts maps) and see if it improves your memory as a listener.

Chapter 5: Selecting a Topic and Purpose

Activity 5.1: Identifying Speech Subjects, Topics, and Goal/Purposes

Summary: The focus of this activity is to give you practice with the speech terms "subject," "topic," and "speech goals or purposes." To gain a better understanding of the distinctions among the terms, you will practice identifying each of the elements in a speech from **InfoTrac**. You will also learn more about the variety of search options in **InfoTrac**.

The speech you will use is **"But Professor, What Are the Humanities for? Creating a Full Human Being" by John Rodden** (March 15, 2002).

1. To locate this speech, you will use the option of locating a specific journal or magazine rather than using a search term. First, click on **"PowerTrac."** Then go to the "entry box" drop down box display. Go down the list of index options until you come to "Journal Name." Click and then in the "entry box" where you usually type the search term, type the journal name. In this case, type "Vital Speeches" and then click on search. Once this is done, go to Search Results and click on "View." You will then get a list of all the articles **InfoTrac** has available in that journal. They are arranged in order of publication, with the most recent articles first. The article "But Professor, What are The Humanities For?" is NOT in the most recent 20 articles displayed. So at the end of the first 20 citations, you will need to click on "Next Page" and continue to look down the list until you locate the article. If the article is not in the second set of citations, then again click on "Next Page" until you locate it (*hint: use the date of the speech to help you*).

2. Read the entire speech before you answer the questions. However, as you read, you may want to mark or make notes on what you think the "subject," "topic," and "goals," or "purposes" are.

3. What is the broad SUBJECT Rodden chose for his speech?

What is the SPEECH TOPIC Rodden chose for his speech?

Is this topic a good fit with the audience? The speaker? The setting /occasion? Support your answers.

_____

_____

_____

4. What is the GENERAL GOAL or GENERAL PURPOSE for the speech? To INFORM (   ) or to PERSUADE (   )?

Give reasons for your answer.

_____

_____

_____

5. What is the SPECIFIC GOAL or SPECIFIC PURPOSE the speaker has chosen for the audience?

_____

_____

5.2 Selecting a Topic and Availability of Information

Summary: After a speaker has tested a potential topic against criteria such as: fit of topic to assignment/context; relevancy of topic for audience; speaker's knowledge about topic; and speaker's interest in topic, it is often useful to check on availability of research material before narrowing the topic and finalizing the specific purpose and thesis. In this exercise, you will do a preliminary **InfoTrac** search of a tentative topic to check on how available outside information is on your topic. You will also find that you are learning more about using **InfoTrac** efficiently as you do the search.

1. Write down a tentative topic you might use for your next assigned speech (e.g., "teen pregnancy"). Make sure that your topic fits the requirements for an acceptable speech topic.

_____

2. Think of several (at least two) synonyms or alternate terms for the topic you have written in #1 that you might use when searching for information.

_____

_____

3. Begin your **InfoTrac** search by first using the "Subject Guide" in **EasyTrac**. You may want to look at the subdivisions of the subject. It may be useful to also use the same search term using the "Key Term" option. Record how many **periodical references** are matches with your search term(s).

Search Term 1_____   Number of Hits

Search Term 2_____   Number of Hits

Search Term 3_____   Number of Hits

4. For each successful search term, look at the titles of the first 20 articles and mark any sources that appear to be promising; scan the articles you have marked. You may want to print a list of marked articles for future reference.

5. Use what you have observed about available information on the topic and subtopics to help you decide on your narrowed topic, specific goal, and thesis for a speech assignment.

Activity 5.3: Browsing for Potential Speech Topics

Summary of Activity: When you find yourself in the position of just not being able to come up with a topic for a speech assignment, you may want to "prime the pump" by browsing through some current periodicals. This activity gives you practice in electronically leafing through periodicals listed on **InfoTrac** that may help you bring to the surface topics that will meet the criteria for selecting a speech topic.

1. Begin by brainstorming your previous interests and experiences. Write down subjects under the following categories.

Vocation/Major	**Hobbies/Leisure Activities**
_____	_____
_____	_____

Current Events/Issues	**Previous Knowledge/Expertise**
_____	_____
_____	_____

2. You will locate titles of magazines that focus on the subject areas you have identified under #1. Your instructor may be able to provide you with a printed list of all magazines or journals found in **InfoTrac**.

You can also find a list of magazines that focus on your specific area by going to the **PowerTrac** option. As you did in Activity 5.1, click on **PowerTrac** then go to the "Search Index." This time select "Journal Name **List** (jn=)."

Next, in the entry box, type one of the subjects you have listed above. For example, if under Hobbies/Leisure Activities, you have listed "sports," then try "sports" as your search term to locate magazines that specialize in sports coverage. If you search is successful, you will be able to view a list of magazines that cover your interest area. Write down one or two magazine titles for each.

Vocation/Major	**Hobbies/Leisure Activities**
_____	_____
_____	_____

(continued on next page)

Current Events/Issues	**Previous Knowledge/Expertise**
_____	_____
_____	_____

3. Here are the instructions to help you browse through specific issues of magazines by looking at the titles of article that may suggest speech topics to you.

To look at a specific magazine on **InfoTrac**, click on the **PowerTrac** option. Again, your first step in **PowerTrac** is to "Choose a Search Index." Go down the list of options to "Journal Name" (jn) and click. Type in the name of any magazine from **Infotrac** that you would like to use to scan the article titles.

You will be told how many articles are on file from that magazine. You obviously do not want to look at several thousand articles. Fortunately, the most recent articles are listed first. View the first 20 articles. To complete scanning the titles of all the articles in that issue of the magazine (check the dates on the articles), you may need to call up the "Next Page" that includes the next 20 articles.

Browse through at least one issue of two different magazines looking for speech topic ideas.

4. Write down any subjects that are either possible speech topics or topics that were triggered in your mind by scanning the article topics. If you find articles that might be useful for one of the topics you have found, be sure to print a copy of the source.

Possible Speech Topics:

_____

_____

_____

_____

CHAPTER 6: Researching Your Speech in the Information Age

Activity 6.1: Practice Using InfoTrac to Research a Speech

Summary of Activity: You will do a practice search for information on the speech topic of "military airplane safety" using **InfoTrac** in order to become familiar with the functions and resources available on **InfoTrac.**

Using EasyTrac

1. Go into the **InfoTrac** system. You will find that there are two levels of **InfoTrac**: **EasyTrac** and **PowerTrac**. For this activity begin with **EasyTrac**. Before you conduct your search, first click on "Help Search" to find instructions on how to search **EasyTrac**. Read the instructions carefully. You may want to print a copy of "Searching in **EasyTrac**" so you will have the directions easily available.

2. Choose the "Subject Guide" option. Type the term "airplanes" into the search entry box and click on "Search."

3. From your search results, view at least one **newspaper article** and one **periodical.** Write down the **titles** of these two sources.

Newspaper Article _____

Periodical _____

4. How many periodical sources did this initial search produce? _____

5. View the list and scan the titles of the first 10 periodical articles. Print three that seem most relevant to airline safety.

6. Now look at the "Related Subjects" for "airplanes". Choose two that would be relevant to the speech topic of "military aircraft" and list them below.

_____

_____

7. While still in **EasyTrac**, select the "Keywords" option. This time use the search term "airplanes and military." How many hits did you get? _____ Were the first 10 articles the same as those from the subject search?

Using PowerTrac

1. Click on the icon for **PowerTrac**. Then click on "PowerTrac Help." Read this section carefully and make a print copy if you desire.

2. Choose the search index "ke" for "keyword." First enter the term "Airplanes." How many hits did you get?_____ Scan the first ten articles. Were they the same as those you found in **EasyTrac**?

_____

3. You will now refine your search by using a search expression. Type "airplanes and military and safety" into the search box. How many hits did you get? _____.

4. Scan the titles of the articles and note how the sources are now more closely related to the speech topic.

Activity 6.2: Issues Related to Conducting E-mail Interviews

Summary of Activity: You will read two articles from **Infotrac** about the pros and cons of using e-mail rather than face-to-face interviews. You will then relate the articles to your information search when researching a speech.

1. Locate the articles **"Keyboard One-on-One" by Lenore Wright** and **"A Critical Exploration of Face-to-Face Interviewing vs. Computer-Mediated Interviewing" by Carolyn Folkman Curasi** (*hint: use the search term "interviewing and e-mail"*).

2. Skim the article **"A Critical Exploration..."** then locate the section titled "Sampling Issues" and write down three possible **problems or disadvantages** of using e-mail interviews as opposed to the face-to-face or phone interviews that are discussed in the article.

A._____

B._____

C._____

3. Read the article **"Keyboard One-on-One"** and write down three **benefits** of using e-mail interviews that are discussed in the article.

A._____

B._____

C._____

4. Referring to the article **"Keyboard One-on-One,"** locate the section titled "Tips from the Pros" and write down three of the tips provided that you think will help you most in conducting interviews.

A._____

B._____

C._____

Activity 6.3: Guidelines for Reliable Internet Information

Summary: You will read an article from **InfoTrac** that provides valuable information you can use to address both the problems of quantity and quality of information from the Internet.

Locate, make a copy of, and read **"Evaluating & Using Web-based Resources" by Glen Bull, Gina Bull, Kara Dawson, and Cheryl Mason** (*hint: use "internet and research and evaluating" in PowerTrac as your search term.*)

1. Why do the authors of the article believe that teachers who limit the number of sources their students may use from the web as opposed to the number of print sources are making a poor choice?

_____

_____

_____

2. How do the authors recommend reducing the gigantic number of hits a student may get on a topic when searching the web?

_____

_____

_____

3. What should be the basis for whether a source is "suspect or unreliable"? Mark the one best answer.

      A. just by being on the web, a source is suspect and may be unreliable

      B. any information not in print is suspect and may be unreliable

      C. information that has not undergone editorial review is suspect and may be unreliable.

Briefly explain what "editorial review" means.

_____

_____

4. Classify the following Internet sources as to whether they are: "likely to be reliable," or "likely to be unreliable." Mark highly reliable sources with an "R" and less reliable sources with a "U."

_____Web sites of public television and commercial news networks

_____Web sites of commercial companies

_____ Web sites of institutional authority such as *New York Times, Consumer Reports,* major research laboratories

_____ Web sites set up for specific courses by graduate students

_____ sources that lack internal consistency (contradictions within the information)

_____ The Drudge Report

_____ the edu. Domain (only on educational servers)

5. Based on your reading, write what you believe are the **two** most important guidelines for finding information from the Internet that is accurate. You may use information both from your text and this article.

_____

_____

6. Write down the Internet address of the Modern Language Association and the American Psychological Association web sites that give information about appropriate methods of citing web sources in papers or bibliographies for speeches.

MLA _____

APA _____

Activity 6.4: Researching YOUR Speech Topic

Summary of Activity: You will conduct an **InfoTrac** search to find information for a speech you are preparing.

1. List your speech topic and tentative speech goal statement or thesis statement.

Topic: _____

Tentative Goal/Thesis Statement: _____

_____

2. Make a list of search terms you think would be useful in locating information on your topic.

Search Terms: _____

_____

Make a note of which term(s) were most helpful. _____

_____

3. By the time you complete this activity, you should have a list of several usable sources that you can use in preparing your speech. You should record the following information for each item you select: **(1) Name of Author, (2) Title of Article, (3) Title of Book or Magazine, (4) Date of Publication**. Before you make your list, check with your instructor to see if any additional information is required, or if you are to use a specific format for your list of sources.

4. Using **EasyTrac,** locate **periodical sources** (e.g. magazines, journals) and that have useful information on your speech topic. Do both a **subject search** and a **keyword search**. Record the sources you select on the List of Sources.

5. If you need to narrow your search because of too many hits or information that does not quite fit, switch to **PowerTrac** to locate **periodical sources**.

List of Sources
Periodical Sources

_____

_____

_____

_____

_____

_____

_____

_____

7. If you have not found at least **six** usable sources, go back and search again using additional search terms.

8. Print copies of articles from your **List of Sources** that you will use in preparing your speech.

CHAPTER 7: Using Supporting Materials

Activity 7.1: Identifying Types of Support Material

Summary: You will locate and read two speeches found on **Infotrac**. You will practice identifying specific categories of support materials that the speakers have used in their speeches.

1. Locate and print a copy of the speech printed in *Vital Speeches*, February 15, 2001, "**From Couch Potato To 50 and Fit" by William D. Novelli** *(hint: use the speaker's full name as your search term.)*

> A. In this speech you will be looking for examples of the speaker's use of two types of support materials: **(1) examples (sometimes called specific instances, illustrations or narratives)** and **(2) definitions**. As you read the speech, mark and label all examples and definitions you find.

> B. Go back to the examples and record the location (e.g. middle of page 4 or third paragraph page 7) of at least one use of the following types of examples (instances). You may use the same example in more than one "example" category.

Real/Factual Example: Location_____

Hypothetical Example: Location _____

Brief Example: Location_____

Extended/Detailed Example: Location _____

Of the examples you selected, which did you think was most effective and why?

_____

_____

> C. Now look at the definitions you marked. Choose and record the location of comparisons that fit the following categories. You may use the same definition in more than one definition category.

Reflects Speaker's "Personal" Definition: Location _____

Based on a Source Other than Speaker: Location _____

Uses Synonyms and/or Antonyms: Location _____

Uses Example and/or Comparison: Location _____

2. Locate and make a copy of the speech published in *Vital Speeches,* January 15, 2001, **"Keeping Freddie Krueger in the Closet" by Rob Lee** (*hint: use the speaker's full name as your search term.*)

      A. In this speech you will be looking for examples of four types of support materials: **(1) comparison (sometimes referred to as comparison/contrast), (2) facts, (3) statistics, and (4) opinions/quotations**. As you read the speech text, mark and label all examples of comparison, facts, statistics, and expert opinions or quotations you find.

      B. Now look again at the comparisons you marked. Choose and record the location of comparisons that fit the following categories.

Literal Comparison: Location_____

Figurative Comparison: Location _____

Of the comparisons Rob Lee used in his speech, which one did you think was the most effective and why?

_____

_____

_____

      C. Choose your favorite example from each category and record the location in the speech text of each.

Fact: Location _____

Statistical/Numerical Information: Location_____

Expert Opinion/Quotation: Location_____

3. Based on the use of support materials in these two speeches, which type of support material do you think is most effective at keeping or retaining **listener interest**?

_____

Again, based on these two speeches, which type(s) of support material(s) do you think is(are) most effective in leading to acceptance of the **speaker's viewpoint**?

_____

Activity 7.2: Testing Support Materials

Summary of Activity: Using a set of questions developed by Clella Jaffa in the public speaking textbook, *Public Speaking: Concepts and Skills for a Diverse Society,* you will evaluate specific support materials from the two speeches used in **Activity 7.1**.

1. If you have not done so already, locate and print a copy of the speech printed in *Vital Speeches,* February 15, 2001, **"From Couch Potato to 50 and Fit" by William D. Novelli** *(hint: se the speaker's full name as your search term).*

A. Test the **examples/instances** from the speech by answering the following two questions:

(1) Are these examples representative or typical? That is, do they represent normal people or typical institutions in the population being discussed, or are they extreme cases?

_____

(2) Are these examples sufficient? Are there enough cases presented to support the major ideas adequately?

_____

B. Test the **definitions** from the speech by answering the following question.

(1) Has the speaker's interjection of a personal interpretation into definitions made the accuracy of those definitions open to question? In what ways?

_____

2. If you have not done so already, locate and make a copy of the speech published in *Vital Speeches,* January 15, 2001, **"Keeping Freddie Krueger in the Closet" by Rob Lee** (*hint: use the speaker's full name as your search term.*)

A. Test the **comparisons** from the speech by answering the following questions.

(1) In the **literal** comparisons, are the two items alike in essential details?

_____

(2) In the **figurative** comparisons, are the comparisons clear and do they make sense? Can the listeners make the necessary connection of ideas?

_____

B. Test the **facts** from the speech by answering the following questions. If the speaker has failed to provide the information you need to answer the questions, note that.

(1) Are the facts accurate? Are they verified by more than one observer or source?

_____

(2) Are the facts up to date? Do they reflect contemporary reality?

_____

(3) Has the speaker provided the source of the facts? Is it a reliable source?

_____

C. Test the **statistical/ numerical** support by answering the following questions. Again, indicate if the speaker has failed to provide necessary information for you to answer the questions.

(1) Is the source of the numbers given? Is it a source without a vested interest?

_____

(2) Are the numbers up to date?

_____

C. Test the **testimony/quotations** in the speech by answering the following questions.

(1) Does the person have expertise in the subject under discussion? Is the person recognized as an expert by others?

_____

(2) Is the opinion typical or representative of others like the source?

_____

Activity 7.3: Making Numbers and Statistics Accessible and Meaningful to the Audience.

Summary: You will study the numbers and statistics used in a speech found through **Infotrac** to identify if the speaker has treated and presented numbers and statistics in a manner that makes them easy for the audience to take in and understand.

1. Locate and make a copy of the speech published in *Vital Speeches*, January 1, 2001, **"The Rap of Change" by Suzanne Morse** (*hint: use speaker's full name as your search term*).

2. As you read, mark the numerical and statistical support the speaker has used in the speech.

3. Analyze the numerical and statistical information used in this speech.

Did the speaker treat and present the numbers and statistics so that the audience could easily grasp and understand them?

_____

Did the numerical and statistical information contribute to, or take away from, the effectiveness of the speech?

_____

4. Create a list of the strategies the speaker used to make the numerical and statistical support accessible and meaningful to the audience, including either how the speaker adjusted to difficult or complex numerical support/statistics, or made the information interesting to the audience.

_____

_____

_____

_____

5. From the list of strategies you created in #4, choose two or three strategies you will use to help your audience understand the numerical support/statistics in your next speech.

_____

_____

_____

CHAPTER 8: Analyzing and Adapting to Audiences

Activity 8.1: Identifying Type of Audience

Summary of Activity: For each of the following speeches from **Infotrac**, you will do a brief assessment of the type of audience and the special audience problems the speaker would need to address because of the uniqueness of the audience.

1. If you have not already done so, locate and make a copy of the **first page** of the speech, **"Keeping Freddie Kreuger in the Closet" by Rob Lee** (*hint: use the speaker's full name as your search term*). Note this speech was used in **Activities 7.1 and 7.2** so you may already have a copy.

A. What is the speaker's position or area of expertise?

_____

B. Identify the group that makes up the audience.

_____

C. Based on the information given about speaker and audience, answer the following questions. Your responses will be only general assumptions, and different students may have different thoughts.
(1) The audience is: captive ( ) or volunteer ( ).

(2) The audience will be: very interested ( ), somewhat interested ( ), have little/no interest ( ).

(3) The audience will be: very friendly ( ), neutral ( ), hostile ( ), a mixture ( ).

(4) The audience has: similar backgrounds ( ), different backgrounds ( ), a mixture of backgrounds ( ).

(5) The audience's attitude toward the speaker will be: positive ( ), negative ( ), mixed ( ).

(6) What do you think will be this speaker's biggest challenge in adapting the speech to this audience?

_____

2. Now locate and copy the **first page** of **"Coerced Abstinence" by Joseph D. McNamara** (*hint: use the speaker's full name as the search term*).

A. What is the speaker's position or area of expertise?

_____

B. Identify the group that makes up the audience.

_____

C. Based on the information given about speaker and audience, answer the following questions. Your responses will be only general assumptions, and different students may have different thoughts.
(1) The audience is: captive ( ) or volunteer ( ).

(2) The audience will be: very interested ( ), somewhat interested ( ), have little/no interest ( ).

(3) The audience will be: very friendly ( ), neutral ( ), hostile ( ), a mixture ( ).

(4) The audience has: similar backgrounds ( ), different backgrounds ( ), a mixture of backgrounds ( ).

(5) The audience's attitude toward the speaker will be: positive ( ), negative ( ), mixed ( ).

(6) What do you think will be this speaker's biggest challenge in adapting the speech to this audience?

_____

3. The next speech is **"Tony Orlando Speaks From Experience."** You just need to copy the first page (*hint: use the term "Tony Orlando" for your search*).

A. What is the speaker's position or area of expertise?

_____

B. Identify the group that makes up the audience.

_____

C. Based on the information given about speaker and audience, answer the following questions. Your responses will be only general assumptions, and different students may have different thoughts.
(1) The audience is: captive ( ) or volunteer ( ).

(2) The audience will be: very interested ( ), somewhat interested ( ), have little/no interest ( ).

(3) The audience will be: very friendly ( ), neutral ( ), hostile ( ), a mixture ( ).

(4) The audience has: similar backgrounds ( ), different backgrounds ( ), a mixture of backgrounds ( ).

(5) The audience's attitude toward the speaker will be: positive ( ), negative ( ), mixed ( ).

(6) What do you think will be this speaker's biggest challenge in adapting the speech to this audience?

_____

4. Now locate and copy the first page of **"Education or Eyeballs"** by **John J. Brennan** (*hint: use the speaker's full name as search term*).

A. What is the speaker's position or area of expertise?

_____

B. Identify the group that makes up the audience.

_____

C. Based on the information given about speaker and audience, answer the following questions. Your responses will be only general assumptions, and different students may have different thoughts.
(1) The audience is: captive ( ) or volunteer ( ).

(2) The audience will be: very interested ( ), somewhat interested ( ), have little/no interest ( ).

(3) The audience will be: very friendly ( ), neutral ( ), hostile ( ), a mixture ( ).

(4) The audience has: similar backgrounds ( ), different backgrounds ( ), a mixture of backgrounds ( ).

(5) The audience's attitude toward the speaker will be: positive ( ), negative ( ), mixed ( ).

(6) What do you think will be this speaker's biggest challenge in adapting the speech to this audience?

_____

Activity 8.2: College Audience Makeup and Attitudes

Summary of Activity: In the classroom, you will be speaking to fellow college students. This activity will give you experience in finding out what studies have shown about the composition of college student population and college student attitudes related to values, beliefs, and controversial issues.

1. First locate and read the article **"Report: U.S. College Population to Increase by 19% Within 20 Years"** (*hint: use search term "U.S. Population Increase"*).

Although this article projects the makeup of college population for the next 20 years, the trends that are reported are already occurring.

Name **three** categories of change in the student population that are reported.

---

2. Here are four articles that report on college student attitudes about issues important to this age group. Locate the four articles. **"College Freshmen Cut Booze ... and Classes" by Andrea Billups, "Health-Risk Behaviors of High School and College Females" by Mary K. Dinger, "College Students' Attitudes Toward Abortion and Commitment to the Issue" by Casey L. Carlton, Eileen S. Nelson, and Priscilla K. Coleman, "Who Doesn't Want To Be a Millionaire? Not Most of These College Students" by Bill Leonard** (*hint: use the search term "college students and attitudes" for all of these articles*).

Read carefully the **first page** of each article to discover information about college student attitudes and answer the following questions.

"College Freshman Cut Booze. . . and Classes"
A. According to the article, how are student attitudes and behaviors toward alcohol and smoking changing?

B. Do you believe the same trends are happening on your campus?

You may want to conduct a survey to verify or reject your perception.

Health-Risk Behaviors of High School and College Females"

A. What are the differences in risky behaviors of college males and females?

_____

_____

B. If you gave a speech on a health-risk behavior such as suicide, failure to use condoms, poor diet, lack of physical activity, how would you need to adapt your speech if there are both male and female college students in your audience?

_____

_____

"College Students' Attitudes Toward Abortion and Commitment to the Issue"

A. Name the factors that influence college students' attitudes toward abortion.

_____

_____

B. How does the influence of these factors on students' attitudes complicate the speaker's job?

_____

_____

"Who Doesn't Want To Be a Millionaire? Not Most of These College Students"

A. What are at least two speech topics that a speaker would need information about student beliefs about their future financial success in order to adapt the speech to the audience?

_____

Activity 8.3: Locating Information About College Audience Attitudes For YOUR Speech Topics

Summary of Activity: You will search **InfoTrac** for college student attitudes on a speech topic of your choice.

1. Choose a topic for a speech you plan to give for which you need to know about audience attitudes toward the topic in order to adapt your speech to your audience.

Speech Topic _____

3. Make a list of possible search terms that focus on the value or issue (e.g. cheating, tax cuts).

Search Terms_____

4. You will need to do a **PowerTrac** search using the following model: **attitudes and (*college students*) and (*your specific value/issue term*).** Here is an example: attitudes and college students and exercise.

5. List articles you found that provide information about college student attitudes and your topic.

_____

_____

_____

6. Read any appropriate articles.

What did you discover about college student attitudes toward your topic?

_____

_____

_____

Activity 8.4: Analysis of Audience Adaptation Techniques

Summary of Activity: You will locate techniques speakers have used to adapt their speeches to their specific audiences. These examples will provide you with models of how you might adapt your own speeches.

1. If you have not already done so, locate and **copy the entire** speech, **"Education or Eyeballs" by John J. Brennan** (*hint: use the speaker's full name as search term*). Note that this speech was used in **Activity 8.1**. At that point, however, you used only the first page.

A. What are some of the features of this audience and situation that the speaker needs to consider when planning the speech?

_____

_____

B. Read the speech and mark the following audience adaptation strategies the speaker uses: **(1) speaks directly to the audience by using personal pronouns (e.g. "you," "we," "I"); (2) refers to shared experiences; (3) refers to recent or current events.**

C. Is this speaker effective at using audience adaptation techniques to build his own credibility as a speaker? Yes (   ) No (   )

Why or Why Not?

_____

_____

_____

D. Is this speaker effective at using audience adaptation techniques to achieve his speech goals? Yes (   ) No (   )

Why or Why Not?

_____

_____

_____

2. Locate and copy **"Tony Orlando Speaks From Experience"** (*hint: use the search term "Tony Orlando"*). Note that this speech was used in **Activity 8.1**. At that point, however, you used only the first page.

A. What are some features of this audience and situation that the speaker needed to consider when planning the speech?

_____

_____

B. Read the speech and mark the following audience adaptation strategies the speaker uses: **(1) speaks directly to the audience by using personal pronouns (e.g. "you," "we," "I"); (2) refers to audience previous knowledge or experience; (3) refers to locations that are important or familiar to audience.**

C. Is this speaker effective at using audience adaptation techniques to build his own credibility as a speaker? Yes ( ) No ( )

Why or Why Not?

_____

_____

D. Is this speaker effective at using audience adaptation techniques to achieve his speech goals? Yes ( ) No ( )

Why or Why Not?

_____

_____

CHAPTER 9: Organizing and Outlining Your Speech

Activity 9.1: Identifying Traditional Speech Organizational Patterns

Summary of Activity: You will locate from **InfoTrac**, copy, and analyze three speeches. The goal is to become more familiar with traditional speech organizational patterns as they are used in actual speeches.

1. Locate and copy **"Education or Eyeballs" by John J. Brennan** (*hint: use the speaker's full name as your search term*). Note that this speech was used in **Activities 8.1 and 8.4** so you may already have a copy.

A. Go through the speech and mark the point at which the introduction ends and the body begins and the point at which the body ends and the conclusion begins.

B. This speaker has not given the listener or reader much obvious help with how the speech is organized. You will probably have to read or at least skim the entire speech before you are able to answer this question. Which category of organization did Brennan use for his main points?

chronological ( )　　topical ( )　　causal ( )　　problem/solution ( )

2. Locate and copy **"The State of the Pet Industry" by Marian Salzman** (*hint: use the speaker's full name as your search term*).

A. Go through the speech and mark the point at which the introduction ends and the body begins and the point at which the body ends and the conclusion begins.

B. Which category of organization did Salzman use for the speech's main points?

chronological ( )　　topical ( )　　causal ( )　problem/solution ( )

C. Explain why you chose the pattern of organization you did.

_____

_____

_____

3. Locate and copy **"The Streets of Life" by William J. Byron** (*hint: use the speaker's full name as your search term*).

This speech is an example of a speaker using a combination of more than one type of organizational pattern. At the most general level (his two main points), Byron uses **problem-solution** organization to address the problem of student development and the roles faculty and administrators can play in it. Look at the section on about page 3 that begins with "I. Becoming Human" where the "solution" begins.

A. Which category of organization does Byron use for the sub-points of the "solution"?

chronological ( )   topical ( )   causal ( )   problem/solution ( )

B. Explain why you chose the pattern of organization you did.

_____

_____

_____

Activity 9.2: Speaker Signposting to Assist the Audience in Following the Speech Organization

Summary of Activity: You will locate and copy a speech from **InfoTrac College Edition** that you will use to identify the language strategies the speaker has used to guide the audience through the speech.

1. Locate and copy **"The Rap of Change" by Suzanne Morse** (*hint: use the full name of the speaker as your search term*). Note that this speech was used in **Activity 7.3** so you may already have a copy.

2. Read the speech and underline or highlight each time the speaker uses language to give a signal to the audience about where they are going in the speech (previews), where they have been (summaries, repetition) where they are in the speech (transitions), or any other word clues to help the audience understand and remember the organization of the speech.

3. What you have underlined is often called "signposting." Some people find signposting very helpful and reassuring in a speech; others claim that signposting just interrupts the flow of the speech.

What is your reaction to Morse's use of signposting in her speech?

_____

_____

_____

_____

Activity 9.3: Additional Organizational Tips

Summary of Activity: You will look at two articles from **InfoTrac College Edition** written for people who do presentations in their professional lives. In addition to other recommendations for improving public speeches, each includes some ideas about organizing speech material that may supplement what you have read in your text about speech organization.

Locate the following articles: **"The Five-Minute Rule for Presentations" by Jacqueline I. Schmidt & Joseph B. Miller** (*hint: use the search term "reason for speaking"*) and **"Stay Cool When Things Get Hot" by Reesa Woolf** (*hint: use the search term "public speaking"*).

1. Scan through **"Stay Cool When Things Get Hot"** to the section titled "Organize Your Thoughts." Read that section carefully.

A. Name one suggestion that focuses on the **general plan of the speech** (outline).

_____

_____

B. Name one suggestion that helps with **internal organization of individual points**.

_____

2. Read the article **"The Five-Minute Rule."**

A. What do you think of the idea of breaking your complete presentation into a series of five-minute talks? How do you think you might incorporate this suggestion into your next in-class presentation?

_____

_____

B. Scan the article to find the paragraph that begins "The five-minute-rule helps speakers limit ideas..." Reflect on this idea that you should focus on asking yourself what the audience needs to know rather than what is important. What can you do in your next in-class presentation to keep your audience in mind as you prepare and deliver your speech?

_____

_____

_____

CHAPTER 10: Organizing and Outlining Introductions and Conclusions

Activity 10.1: Analysis of Introductions

Summary of Activity: You will locate four different speeches on **InfoTrac**, print copies of each speech and then use the manuscripts to analyze the components of each speech's introduction.

Speech 1: "The Rap of Change" by Suzanne Morse (*hint: use the complete name of the speaker as your search term*).

1. Locate the speech on **InfoTrac** and make a copy. Note this speech was used for **Activities 7.3 and 9.2** so you may already have a copy. You will use approximately the first three pages for this activity.

2. On your copy of the speech, mark the **attention-getting section** of the speaker's introduction.

Which category/categories of attention-getting techniques does this represent?

_____

Evaluate the effectiveness of this speaker's choice of attention-getter. Be prepared to defend your evaluation.

_____

_____

_____

3. Now highlight or underline on the speech manuscript information from the speech introduction that functions to **establish speaker credibility and rapport with audience**.

Evaluate the effectiveness of this speaker's choices for establishing her credibility and rapport with the audience.

_____

_____

_____

4. Locate and mark the speaker's announced plan for the speech (this may be goal statement, thesis, or preview).

How would you change the announced plan for the speech to make it more helpful for the audience?

_____

_____

Speech 2: "'The Survivor' Is a Sham" by Jeffery L. Zelms (*hint: use the full name of the speaker as your search term*).

1. Locate the speech on **InfoTrac** and print a copy. You will use approximately the first two-and-a-half pages for this activity.

2. On your copy of the speech, mark the **attention-getting section** of the speaker's introduction.

Which category/categories of attention-getting techniques does this represent?

_____

Evaluate the effectiveness of this speaker's choice of attention-getter. Be prepared to defend your evaluation.

_____

_____

_____

3. Now highlight or underline on the speech manuscript information from the speech introduction that functions to **establish speaker credibility, rapport with audience, and significance or relevancy of topic for audience.**

Evaluate the effectiveness of this speaker's choices for establishing his credibility, rapport with the audience, and significance/relevancy of topic for audience.

_____

_____

4. Locate and mark the speaker's announced plan for the speech (may be goal statement, thesis, or preview).

How would you change the announced plan for the speech to make it more helpful for the audience?

_____

Speech 3: "A Decade of Difference" by Jack Guynn (*hint: use the full name of the speaker for your search term*).

1. Locate the speech on **InfoTrac** and print a copy. Use approximately the first one-and-one-half pages for this activity.

2. On your copy of the speech, mark the **attention-getting section** of the speech introduction.

Which category/categories of attention-getting techniques does this represent?

_____

Evaluate the effectiveness of this speaker's choice of attention-getter. Be prepared to defend your evaluation.

_____

_____

_____

3. Now highlight or underline on the speech manuscript information from the speech introduction that functions to **establish speaker credibility and rapport with audience.**

Evaluate the effectiveness of this speaker's choices for establishing speaker credibility and rapport with the audience.

_____

_____

_____

4. Locate and mark the speaker's announced plan for the speech (may be goal statement, thesis, or preview).

How would you change the announced plan for the speech to make it more helpful for the audience?

_____

_____

Speech 4: "Urban Universities" by David l. Stocum (*hint: use the full name of the speaker as your search term*).

1. Locate the speech on **InfoTrac** and print a copy. You will use the first page of the speech.

2. On your copy of the speech, mark the **attention-getting section** of the speaker's introduction.

Which category/categories of attention-getting techniques does this represent?

_____

Evaluate the effectiveness of this speaker's choice of attention-getter. Be prepared to defend your evaluation.

_____

_____

_____

3. Now highlight or underline on the speech manuscript information from the speech introduction that functions to **establish speaker credibility, rapport with audience, and background of topic for audience.**

Evaluate the effectiveness of this speaker's choices for establishing her credibility, rapport with the audience, and background of topic for audience.

_____

_____

_____

4. Locate and mark the speaker's announced plan for the speech (this may be goal statement, thesis, or preview).

Evaluate how helpful the announced plan of the speech is for the audience.

_____

Activity 10.2: Analysis of Conclusions

Summary of Activity: You will locate four different speeches from **InfoTrac**, make print copies of each speech and then use the manuscripts to analyze the components of each speech's conclusion. (**NOTE: These are the same speeches that were used in the previous activity. You will be able to use the same copies of the speeches if you completed that activity.**) (Hint: *If you have not yet located these speeches, use the full name of each speaker as your search term*).

Speech 1: "The Rap of Change" by Suzanne Morse.

1. Locate the speech on **InfoTrac** and make a copy if you have not already done so. You will use the last page of the speech for this activity.

2. On the copy, mark where the conclusion starts.

What statement did the speaker use to alert the audience to the beginning of the conclusion?

_____

3. Did the speaker include a summary of the main points? _____ If so, underline or highlight the summary.

4. Highlight or underline the speaker's closing remarks that function to **refocus thought, end with impact, or hit home**.

Evaluate these final comments of the speaker for effectiveness.

_____

_____

_____

Speech 2: "'The Survivor' Is a Sham" by Jeffery L. Zelms.

1. Locate the speech on **InfoTrac** and make a copy if you have not already done so. You will use the last page of the manuscript for this activity.

2. On the copy, mark where the conclusion starts.

What statement did the speaker use to alert the audience to the beginning of the conclusion?

_____

3. Did the speaker include a summary of the main points?_____ If so, underline or highlight the summary.

4. Highlight or underline the speaker's closing remarks that function to **refocus thought, end with impact, or hit home**.

Evaluate these final comments of the speaker for effectiveness.

_____

_____

_____

Speech 3: "A Decade of Difference" by Jack Guynn.

1. Locate the speech on **InfoTrac** and make a copy if you have not already done so. You will use page 8 of the manuscript for this activity.

2. On the copy, mark where the conclusion starts. (For this speech, you may find that different students have different opinions.)

What statement did the speaker use to alert the audience to the beginning of the conclusion?

_____

3. Did the speaker include a summary of the main points?_____ If so, underline or highlight the summary.

4. Highlight or underline the speaker's closing remarks that function to **refocus thought, end with impact, or hit home**.

Evaluate these final comments of the speaker for effectiveness.

_____

_____

Speech 4: "Urban Universities" by David L. Stocum.

1. Locate the speech on **InfoTrac** and make a copy if you have not already done so. You will use approximately the last two pages of the manuscript for this activity.

2. On the copy, mark where the conclusion starts.

What statement did the speaker use to alert the audience to the beginning of the conclusion?

_____

3. Did the speaker include a summary of the main points?_____ If so, underline or highlight the summary.

4. Highlight or underline the speaker's closing remarks that function to **refocus thought, end with impact, or hit home**.

Evaluate these final comments of the speaker for effectiveness.

_____

_____

_____

Activity 10.3: Motivating the Audience to Listen Because of Relevancy Presented in Introduction

Summary of Activity: Use **InfoTrac** to locate information about the following three speech topics that could be shared with the audience in the introduction to demonstrate that the topic is important and has significance for them. Record information you could use to establish topic relevancy in a speech on each of the following topics.

Speech Topic 1: Skin Damage from the Sun (*hint: you may want to try both "skin damage" and "sun damage" as search terms*).

_____

_____

_____

_____

_____

Speech Topic 2: Affirmative Action

_____

_____

_____

_____

_____

Speech Topic 3: DVD Players

_____

_____

_____

_____

Activity 10.4: Practice Speech Introductions

Summary of Activity: Using a speech topic of your choice, you will prepare three introductions for the speech. Use a **different attention-getter for each of the three introductions**. You may use the same or similar information to complete each introduction. You may be asked to stand in front of the class and present one or more of your introductions.

For example using the topic "Pleistocene Diets," the speaker might begin the first introduction by telling a story of a day in the life of a caveman (or woman) centering around the typical meals these hunters and gatherers collected and ate. The second introduction might begin with the startling statement that researchers from South Africa and France have just discovered that a major source of protein in early humans' diets was termites, a source modern advocates of the Pleistocene Diet might not find either appealing or available at the supermarket. For the third introduction the speaker could ask the questions: Would you like to find a diet that not only promotes weight loss, would allow you to live a long and healthy life, and may have contributed to the development of superior brain size in humans?

1. Choose a speech topic to use for this assignment.

_____

2. Use **InfoTrac** to find suitable information on your topic such as narratives, startling statements/facts, or quotations.

Write the name(s) of the article(s) you are using as source(s).

_____

_____

3. Write the three introductions.

Introduction 1   Type of Attention-getter _____

_____

_____

_____

_____

_____

_____

_____

_____

_____

_____

Introduction 2   Type of Attention-getter_____

_____

_____

_____

_____

_____

_____

_____

_____

_____

_____

_____

Introduction 3   Type of Attention-getter_____

_____

_____

_____

_____

_____

_____

_____

_____

_____

_____

_____

CHAPTER 11: Visual Aids

Activity 11.1: Creating Visual Aids for Statistical/Numerical Data

Summary of Activity: You will work with the text of a speech from **InfoTrac** to practice designing visual aids to make statistics and numbers clearer and more memorable for the audience.

1. Locate and copy "**How America Shops 2000**" by Wendy Liebmann (*hint: use the speaker's full name as the search term*).

2. In the speech text, find and mark **two sets of data** that could be presented by using visual aids. Look for examples that the audience really needs a visual presentation to easily understand and remember the information.

3. Make a **sketch** of a chart or graph for each of the data sets that illustrates the numerical information in such a way that the audience will be able to have almost instantaneous understanding of the data.

DATA SET 1:

DATA SET 2:

Now that you have a draft of a visual aid, consider whether another graphic format (bar, pie, line) would have been more appropriate for this data.

An alternative graphic format for this data would be _____

Activity 11.2: Issues about the Use of Computer-generated Visual Aids

Summary of Activity: You will locate an article about the problems associated with the use of software such as PowerPoint for public speaking presentations and reflect on possible ways to more effectively use such software and other visual aids.

1. Locate and read **"Missing the Point: How PowerPoint May be Sucking the Life Out of Your Sales Presentation" by Mark McMaster** (*hint: use "presentation* and PowerPoint" as your search term in **PowerTrac**).

2. McMaster asserts that "When audience members are spending most of their time with their eyes glued to the screen, they're ignoring the speaker--and part of the purpose of presenting to a group is to establish trust and confidence through your delivery." How often have you been in attendance of a speech that had you reading more than listening?

_____

3. Locate and list the two rules that users of PowerPoint should remember. Describe the ways in which you have seen these rules violated in presentations you have observed.

_____

_____

_____

4. The article posits that PowerPoint is a visual medium and should be used to illustrate points, not make them redundant. Describe one way you might use PowerPoint to accomplish this task in an upcoming speech.

_____

_____

_____

_____

Activity 11.3: Information about Technology Used in Creating and Showing Visual Aids

Summary of Activity: You will locate and read an article that presents a summary of computer technology available to help you create professional-looking visual aids fairly simply. You will then consider what resources you have available and what approaches appeal to you.

1. Locate and read **"High-Tech Show and Tell" by Pam Sloane** (*hint: in **PowerTrac**, use the term "presentation* and PowerPoint"*).

2. Investigate what resources are available on your campus. You may have a computing assistance center that you can call or visit. Which of the techniques from the article would you have the resources to use?

_____

_____

_____

_____

Activity 11.4: Advanced Techniques for Computer Software Slide Shows

Summary of Activity: This activity is especially applicable for students who are already using basic computer software applications to prepare visual aids for their speeches. You are to find one or more articles in the publication *Presentations* that present suggestions and specific directions for adding more impact and effectiveness to your presentations through the use of computer mediated visuals.

1. Locate, copy, and read one or more articles that are relevant to advancing your knowledge of computer-mediated graphics. To locate these articles, you will use the option of locating a specific journal or magazine rather than using a search term. First, click on "**PowerTrac**." Then go to the "Search Index" drop down box display. Go down the list of index options until you come to "Journal Name." Click and then in the "entry box" where you usually type the search term, type the journal name. In this case, type "Presentations." Go to Search Results and click on "View." You will then get a list of all the articles **InfoTrac** has available in that journal. They are arranged in order of publication, with the most recent articles first.

2. As you read each article, highlight or mark any suggestions that rely on equipment and/or software that is available to you.

3. Look over the list of possible techniques you have marked. Choose and write down at least three techniques you will include in your preparation of visual aids for an upcoming speech.

Techniques:

_____

_____

_____

CHAPTER 12: Practicing Speech Wording (Language)

Activity 12.1: Language, Culture, and Identity

Summary of Activity: Two articles from **InfoTrac College Edition** provide resource information about the relationship of language, culture, and identity with cultural groups. You will consider the implications of dialects, code-switching, and appropriate language in the public speaking classroom.

The articles that will be used in this activity are: **" 'I've Called 'em Tom-ah-toes All My Life and I'm Not Going to Change!': Maintaining Linguistic Control Over English Identity in the U.S." by Katharine W. Jones**, and **"It's Time We Rejected the Racial Litmus Test: I Hoped My Sons Wouldn't Have to Prove Their Black Identity. Despite Integration, the Struggle Continues."**

1. Locate **"'I've Called 'em Tom-ah-toes All My Life and I'm Not Going to Change!': Maintaining Linguistic Control Over English Identity in the U.S"** (*hint: use "English language" as your search term and then check the Periodical references*).

This is a report of scholarly research on English immigrants in the U.S. and their use of language to maintain their "Englishness." Although most student who are using this book are probably not English, nor in a classroom with a large number of English students, all students have a "culture" and use language specific to that culture. The article provides a research and theoretical background of the relationship of culture, language, and identity. This is the section of the article you need to concentrate on. Read the first part of the article, approximately pages 1-5. You may stop when you get to "ENGLISH ACCENTS IN ENGLAND" if you wish, or continue on.

Why did the English immigrants cling to their English accents and resist using "Americanisms"?

_____

_____

_____

How is language used to construct and define the different "identities" a person may develop?

_____

_____

_____

2. Locate and read **"It's Time We Rejected the Racial Litmus Test: I Hoped My Sons Wouldn't Have to Prove Their Black Identity. Despite Integration, the Struggle Continues"** (*hint: use "black English" as your search term and then check the Periodical references.*)

From the narrative, point out examples of:

Multiple Cultural Identities_____

_____

Code-switching _____

_____

3. Based on what you have read and thought about in this activity, consider and discuss this question:

Should students in public speaking classes be required to use "Standard English" when giving speeches or should they be allowed to use their "home dialect"? Give reasons for your answer.

_____

_____

_____

_____

Activity 12.2: Avoiding Sexist Language

Summary of Activity: The two articles chosen for this activity present both a summary of the thinking behind the movement toward gender-free language and some suggestions about implement non-sexist language in your speeches.

1. Locate and read **"Sport Management Students' Views on Eliminating Sexist Language" by Janet B. Parks and Mary Ann Roberton** (*hint: use the search term "sexist language."*) and **"Does Alternating Between Masculine and Feminine Pronouns Eliminate Perceived Gender Bias in Text?" by Laura Madson and Robert M. Hessling** (*hint: use the search term "nonsexist language"*). When you read the second article, concentrate on the "INTRODUCTION" and "DISCUSSION" sections—you may skim the rest.

2. What are the reasons for a using gender-free language when giving a speech?

_____

_____

_____

_____

3. Based on the first study, what do students believe are the appropriate approaches to promote the movement from sexist to nonsexist language?

_____

_____

_____

4. Based on the results and discussion from the second study and your personal preference, which technique(s) for avoiding the generic masculine (e.g. "he" "his" for both sexes), do (will) you use when giving your speeches?

_____

_____

_____

Activity 12.3: Identifying Effective Language Strategies

Summary of Activity: You will locate and read a speech from **InfoTrac** that is a good model of using effective language strategies. You will analyze the speaker's language to collect examples of some basic strategies.

1. Locate and make a copy of **"How America Shops 2000" by Wendy Liebmann** (*hint: use the speaker's full name as your search term*). Note this article was used for **Activity 11.1** so you may already have a copy.

2. Use different colored markers or different symbols to mark the language Liebmann uses that fits each of the following strategy categories: **CLEAR** (language that is **concrete, specific, simple, concise**), **VIVID** (figurative language such as metaphors, similes, personification), **EMPHATIC** (placement of words and repetition).

3. Write several of the most effective examples for each category.

Clear:_____

_____

Vivid:_____

_____

Emphatic:_____

_____

CHAPTER 13: Practicing Delivery

Activity 13.1: Regional Pronunciation in Speaking

Summary: You will locate and read an article that provides recent information about trends of pronunciation of words in different regions of North America. You will then apply the information from the article to your own experience with regional pronunciations and appropriate use of regional dialects in the public speaking classroom.

1. Locate and read **"Presenter Behaviors: Actions Often Speak Louder Than Words" by Lillian H. Chaney and Catherine G. Green** (*hint: use "vocalized pauses" as your search term*).

2. Scan the article to find the second sentence in the second paragraph. After reading this sentence, reflect on your experiences in perceiving a speakers' credibility based on their nonverbal behavior. Write down two behaviors you've seen that led to your seeing a person as less credible after s/he began speaking and two behaviors that have increased a different person's credibility after s/he began speaking.

_____

_____

_____

_____

3. Scan the article until you find the section titled "Vocal Characteristics." Scan this section until you find the discussion of pauses. Reflect on your own use of vocalized pauses ("uh, um, like") and the message these pauses may send to people who listen to you speak in a variety of contexts (e.g., in an interview, in a formal presentation, in a conversation with a friend). Write down two or three negatives interpretations of vocalized pauses and one way you might begin to eliminate these behaviors from your speaking repertoire.

_____

_____

_____

_____

_____

Activity 13.2: Using the Body to Communicate Confidence and Power

Summary of Activity: The issue in the article for this activity from **InfoTrac** is the relationship of perceived strength or weakness of the speech delivery of women in business positions and their success. After you read the article, you will answer questions that represent your thinking and evaluation of the author's claims.

1. Locate, print, and read **"You've Got the Power!" by Robyn D. Clarke** (*hint: use "nonverbal communication" as your search term*).

2. Do you agree with the author's claim that many women have a **weak** nonverbal communication style when speaking in public? _____

 Do you agree with the author's claim that women's **weak** nonverbal delivery style is a disadvantage in the professional world? _____

 Do you believe that women should deliberately try to change their nonverbal speech delivery style to demonstrate more confidence and strength? _____

Be ready to provide reasons for your answers.

3. Read over the specific recommendations for confident delivery given in this article. Highlight or underline all the delivery advice that you think is sound for both males and females.

Activity 13.3: Natural Gestures in Public Speaking

Summary: For this activity, you will locate and read an article written for photographers about gestures used by both speakers and listeners that communicate effectively to those who look at the pictures. The advice to photographers also applies to public speakers as they speak and as they observe the gestures of their audience while they are speaking.

1. Locate and read **"Capturing Feelings on Film: Natural Gestures Work Best" by Philip N. Douglis** (*hint: use "gestures" as the search term*).

2. What kinds of messages do natural gestures covey to audiences?

_____

_____

3. Why are planned, programmed gestures usually less effective than natural, spontaneous gestures?

_____

_____

_____

4. The pictures in the article also show gestures used by listeners or audience members. While presenting a speech, do you observe the audience gestures? _____

 5. Is it appropriate for a speaker to adapt to audience response communicated by their gestures while giving a speech?

_____

CHAPTER 14: Principles of Informative Speaking

Activity 14.1: Informative Speaking in the "Information Age"

Summary of Activity: Before looking specifically at informative speeches, you will read a speech found through **InfoTrac** that provides a background for thinking broadly about information in the "Information Age." The article raises issues of potential dangers of focusing on information alone, rather than on communication and knowledge. You will then reflect on and respond to the speaker's ideas.

1. Locate and read **"The Coming Age of Content and Critical Thinking" by Robert L. Dilenschneider** (*hint: use speaker's full name as your search term*).

2. According to Dilenschneider, what are the differences between "information," "knowledge," and "wisdom"?

_____

_____

_____

_____

_____

3. When presenting an Informative Speech, which one or ones of the following should the speaker present to the audience?

information (   ) knowledge (   ) wisdom (   )

Give reasons for your answer.

_____

_____

4. How does the "Information Age" make the informative speaker's job both easier and more difficult?

_____

_____

_____

5. The speaker quotes a university teacher who says," 'We are now focusing more on how to use the tools of communication than we are on how to effectively communicate, ' he complains. 'As a result, we are turning out computer and Internet gurus who can't write and can't think creatively.'"

Do you agree or disagree? Why?

_____

_____

_____

_____

Activity 14.2: Identifying Informative Speeches

Summary of Activity: You will examine three speeches from **InfoTrac** and determine whether each speech carries out a primary goal of **sharing information** or of **persuading** an audience. Then you will reinforce your understanding of the difference between the two speech categories by recording how you made your decisions.

1. Locate and read the three following speeches: **"The Issue of Drug Costs" by Sidney Taurel;** **"Eyes on the Road, Hands on the Wheel" by John F. Smith Jr.** and **"The State of the Pet Industry" by Marian Salzman** (this speech was used in **Activity 9.1**). (*Hint: use the speaker's full name as your search term to locate these speeches*).

2. Mark each speech as either "Informative" or "Persuasive" based on the **primary focus** of the content of the speech and your perception of the **primary goal** of the speaker.

#1: The Issue of Drug Costs _____

#2: Eyes on the Road, Hands on the Wheel _____

#3: The State of the Pet Industry _____

3. Give reasons for your conclusions.

_____

_____

_____

_____

_____

Activity 14.3: Analyzing Informative Approaches and Strategies

Summary of Activity: You will further examine one of the speeches from **Activity 14.2** to discover the speaker's informative approach and use of strategies.

1. If you have not already, locate and copy **"Eyes on the Road, Hands on the Wheel"** by **John F. Smith** (*hint: use the speaker's full name as your search term*).

2. Which **informative approach** has the speaker predominantly used in this speech: **demonstration of a process** (   ); **informative narration** (   ); **explanation of a process or phenomenon** (   )?

3. Locate and evaluate the effectiveness of the speaker's strategies for: **getting and maintaining audience attention; promoting audience understanding; promoting audience memory of speech content**.

Evaluation of **Attention Strategies**:_____

_____

Evaluation of **Understanding Strategies**: _____

_____

Evaluation of **Memory Strategies**: _____

_____

Activity 14.4: Informative Speaking to Counter Misinformation

Summary of Activity: You will read a speech by a spokesperson for a drug company that has as its goal providing information to counter "misinformation" the public has received about drug costs, especially as related to senior citizens. You will notice the strategies the speaker uses and their effectiveness.

1. Locate and read **"The Issue of Drug Costs" by Sidney Taurel** (*hint: an easy way to locate the speech is to use the speaker's full name as your search term*). Note that this speech was used in **Activity 14.2** so you may already have a copy.

2. Did the speaker's use of information effectively counter critics' information about drugs being overpriced?

_____

3. Name at least three strategies Taurel used to counter the misinformation.

_____

_____

_____

CHAPTER 15: Principles of Persuasive Speaking (Reasoning)

Activity 15.1: Identifying the Steps of Monroe's Motivated Sequence in a Speech

Summary of Activity: Through **InfoTrac**, you will locate and read a speech that has used the basic elements of Monroe's Motivated Sequence to organize the speech and enhance persuasion. You will identify each of the steps in the speech and analyze the persuasive techniques that have been used.

1. Locate and copy **"Prize and Embrace What is America" by Farah M. Walters** (*hint: use the speaker's full name as your search term*).

Since this is a fairly long speech, you will be given guidelines about the beginning and end of each step in Monroe's Motivated Sequence.

2. **ATTENTION STEP:** Approximately the first two-and-three-quarters pages are devoted to the Attention Step. This part of the speech ends on about the third page with the paragraph that begins "And yet, in speaking with you today . . . ." On your copy mark where the Attention Step begins and ends.

Answer the following questions about this part of the speech.

A. Find and mark examples of how Walters uses **emotional appeals** to get the audience's attention in the section.

Name two emotions she wants her audience feel. _____

_____

B. As you read the attention step, what did you think the speaker's purpose for the speech might be?

_____

_____

3. **NEED STEP:** The Need Step begins where the Attention Step ends and continues until approximately page 4 with the paragraph that begins: "And so I turn to you this afternoon," mark the beginning and end of this section of the speech in the speech text, then record the following information:

Statement (s) That Identifies What Problem Is: _____

_____

Illustration or Evidence That Supports Problem:_____

_____

_____

_____

4. **SATISFACTION STEP:** (begins where "Need Step" ends and continues until start of "Visualization Step" on approximately page 6)

Connection Between Need and Solution (How does this solution satisfy the need?)

_____

_____

Practicality of Solution (Why will encouraging women to vote work better than appealing to population in general?)

_____

_____

_____

5. **VISUALIZATION STEP:** The Visualization Step for this speech extends from approximately the lower part of page 6, beginning with "Maybe we can build on that new power," to the end of the page.

Name several of the positive "visions" Walters has for the "new era."

_____

_____

Emotional or psychological appeals associated with visualization of task.

_____

_____

6. **ACTION STAGE:** This stage begins with the story about the knight on the last page.

What does Walters ask her audience to do?

_____

What do you think of her choice for action?

_____

_____

_____

Activity 15.2: Identifying and Analyzing Problem/Solution Organization in a Speech

Summary of Activity: You will locate, read and analyze a speech from **InfoTrac** to gain more experience with Problem/Solution Organization of a persuasive speech.

1. Locate and print a copy of **"The Dark Side of Technology" by William N. Joy** (*hint: use the speaker's full name as your search term*). This speech provides of an example of a problem/solution speech in which the primary emphasis is on showing the audience the problem rather than focusing on the solution.

Read the speech looking for (1) how the speaker establishes and analyzes the problem and (2) what solutions the speaker rejects and what solutions the speaker suggests to solve the problem.

Mark the location where the speaker moves from the problem to the solution.

PROBLEM: Answer the following questions about the speaker's development of the problem section.

What is the basic problem? _____

What is the **nature** of the problem? _____

_____

What are the **causes** of the problem? _____

_____

SOLUTION:

What solutions does the speaker recommend? _____

_____

_____

Which **type of persuasive speech** does this represent?

      Conviction Speech (goal is to change or reinforce an audience belief) ( )

      OR **Actuation Speech** (goal is for audience to take action) ( )

Activity 15.3: Modeling Arguments

Summary of Activity: You will model two arguments from a speech using a simplified version of the Toulmin Model.

1. This activity uses the same speech as was used in **Activity 15.2**. If you have not yet done so, locate and print a copy of **"The Dark Side of Technology" by William N. Joy** (*hint: the speech can be located by using the speaker's full name as the search term*).

Argument 1: The central argument of the speech is a **deductive argument** found on about the second page. Identify which statements represent "premises" and which the "general conclusion."

"all practices in these sciences become information" _____

"all information is available" _____

"then clearly the weapon kind of information will be available as well" _____

Argument 2: This **inductive** argument is found approximately on page 4. It is in the paragraph that begins: "The danger with these technologies –GNR—is . . . ." Read the argument and then use the information to complete the following parts of the argument in the model. For data, don't try to write complete sentences or give sources. **You will have to supply the Warrant** based on the Data and Claim given.

DATA (Grounds/Evidence): _____

_____

_____

WARRANT (Logical Connection Between DATA and CLAIM): _____

_____

_____

CLAIM (Conclusion): _____

_____

_____

Argument 3: On approximately page 5, the speaker makes the argument that has as its CLAIM (Conclusion) "we will have to look beyond technical fixes." Locate and write down the DATA that supports this claim and create an appropriate WARRANT.

DATA (Grounds/Evidence): _____

_____

_____

WARRANT (Logical Connection Between DATA and CLAIM): _____

_____

_____

CLAIM (Conclusion): "we will have to look beyond technical fixes"

CHAPTER 16: Speaking at Special Occasions

Activity 16.1: Analyzing Commemorative Speeches

Summary of Activity: You will locate from **InfoTrac** and read two commemorative speeches. Commemorative speeches are often speeches for some special event such as a dedication, commencement or conference. You will analyze each speech to understand better some techniques used in commemorative speeches.

SPEECH #1:
1. Locate and make a copy of **"Being Educators: A Celebration of People" by Martin C. Jischke**, President, Purdue University (*hint: use "commencement address" as your search term*).

2. In your copy of the speech mark the following items:

A. statements that show the speaker **recognizes or acknowledges the occasion,**

B. statements the speaker makes to show **connection or similarity between himself and audience members,**

C. statements that show a **shared history between speaker and audience members,**

D. statements **that "keep the memory of those who have gone before alive,"**

E. statements designed **to inspire.**

F. appropriate use of **humor**

SPEECH #2
1. Locate and make a copy of **"The melting pot: finding solutions to cultural differences" by Luis M. Proenza**. March 1, 2002 (*hint: an easy way to locate this speech is to use EasyTrac, enter the speaker's name into the entry box, and scroll down until you find this speech*).

2. In your copy of the speech mark the following items:

A. statements that show the speaker **recognizes or acknowledges the occasion,**

B. statements the speaker makes to show **connection or similarity between himself and audience members,**

C. statements that show a **shared history between speaker and audience members,**

D. statements that **praise the school/college and graduates**

E. statements **of advice or inspiration** for the graduate's future lives.

Activity 16.2: Analyzing Speeches of Tribute

Summary of Activity: You will be looking at three short eulogies, tribute speeches to someone who has recently died. The focus of the activity is to note the traditional elements of eulogies and to identify effective strategies the speakers use.

1. Locate, copy, and read the following three eulogies: **"From the Heart: Mere Tolerance is Not Enough" by Justin Trudeau; "Eulogy" by Robert Redford** and **"Eulogy" by A. Scott Berg** (*hint: use the search term "eulogy" for all three*).

2. One of the major features of eulogies is to praise the person's **characteristics** and/or **accomplishments**. In all three eulogies, highlight or underline examples of this feature.

3. A danger the speaker faces is that of over-praising and giving an unrealistic picture of a perfect human being.

Mark examples of how the speakers in these examples present a very human picture of the people they eulogize by restrained praise or by showing that those they are praising have **ordinary traits or flaws**.

4. Now locate at least one effective **example** each of the speakers has chosen to show the special attributes of the person.

5. Finally, note and mark any examples of the **eloquent use of language** that stand out in these speeches.

6. Share what you have marked with other class members.

Activity 16.3: Analyzing Speeches of Acceptance

Summary of Activity: You will read two speeches of acceptance. The purpose of the activity is to help you understand the different elements that compose a speech of acceptance and to identify the strategies the speakers use to convey gratitude and sincerity.

1. Locate, print and read the following two speeches of acceptance: **"Audacious grace" by Diana L. Hayes**, and "**Acceptance Speech on Receipt of Financial Engineer of the Year Award" by Emanuel Derman** (*hint: use "award and speech" as your search term*).

2. One of the major purposes of a speech of acceptance is to show gratitude and pleasure for receiving an honor, award, or gift. In both speeches, highlight or underline examples of this feature.

3. In a speech of acceptance, it is important to understand the history and significance of the award. Describe two ways each speech accomplishes the task of indicating to the audience that the recipient understands the importance of the award.

_____

_____

_____

_____

4. Did either speaker use their understanding of the award to remind the audience of larger social issues or to inspire them in some way? If so, provide one example from each speech.

_____

_____

5. Note and mark any examples of the eloquent use of language that stand out in these speeches.

_____

_____

_____

CHAPTER 17: Speaking and Leadership In Small Groups

Activity 17.1: Importance of Small Group Communication in the Professional World

Summary of Activity: You will do a search for information on the importance of groups in the professional world using **InfoTrac**.

1. Go into the **InfoTrac** system, click on **PowerTrac**, scroll to "subject" in the search entry box and enter various search expressions such as "teamwork," "committees," and "groups."

2. What are some of your conclusions about the number of hits relative to the importance of teamwork to your life and career goals?

_____

_____

3. Choose two articles that seem the most interesting and relevant to you and your career goals. Print and read them and describe what you learned about the importance of teamwork. Be sure to include the titles, authors and dates of the articles you read.

_____

_____

_____

Activity 17.2: Leadership Styles

Summary: You will locate and read three articles that present different facets of leadership in groups ranging from competitive sports to nursing to politics. You will have an opportunity to consider the positive and negative aspects of leadership styles.

1. Locate and read the following articles from **InfoTrac**: **"Leadership Styles of Elite Dixie Youth Baseball Coaches" by Greg Bennett and Mark Maneval, "Leadership Effectiveness: How Do You Measure Up?" by Maureen C. Trott and Kim Windsor,** and **"Women as Leaders: Vive la Difference" by Rich Jones and Gary Boulard** (*hint: use "leadership styles" as your search term*).

2. One common way to categorize leadership styles in problem-solving groups is to divide leaders between those who are task-oriented (they focus on the job and getting it done) and person-oriented (they focus on the participation of group members). In general, task-oriented leaders are more autocratic and person-oriented leaders are more democratic. In addition to these two basic styles, the writers and scholars in the articles add other features and use somewhat different labels.

"Leadership Styles of Elite Dixie Youth Baseball Coaches"

Based on the results of the study reported in this article, does the leadership style of the baseball coaches correspond more closely with the **task-oriented style (   )** OR the **person-oriented style (   )**?

Do these results surprise you? _____

What would be the advantages of each style in competitive sports?

_____

_____

_____

"Leadership Effectiveness: How Do You Measure Up?"
Read the first page carefully, and then you may skim the rest of the article.

Which style described here is more closely related to **task-oriented style—transformational leader (   )** or **transactional leader (   )**?

Name one positive aspect of each style.

Transformational Leader _____

Transactional Leader _____

"Women as Leaders: Vive la Difference" (Read both articles.)

With which category does the feminine style of leadership as described in these articles correspond most closely—**task-oriented leader** (   ) or **person-oriented leader** (   )?

On what behaviors or characteristics that were included in the articles did you base you decision?

_____

_____

_____

3. Based on these articles, which style of leadership for problem-solving groups would you recommend? **Task-oriented** (   ) **Person-oriented** (   ) a **combination** of both (   )?

Reasons for your answer:

_____

_____

_____

_____

Activity 17.3: Avoiding Groupthink

Summary: You will print and read two articles that discuss behaviors that promote teamwork and those that lead to groupthink. You will read both articles, identify these behaviors and then discuss ways to achieve a balance between teamwork and groupthink.

1. Locate, copy and read "**What Can You Learn from Enron? How to Know if You Are Creating A Climate of Rule-Breaking**" by JoAnn Barefoot (*hint: use "groupthink" as your textword search term in PowerTrac*) and "**Making Teamwork Work**" by Bob Nelson (*hint: use "teamwork" as your search term in EasyTrac*).

2. From the article "**What Can You Learn**," list and briefly describe the 6 conditions that produce a climate in which serious rule-breaking can occur.

A. _____

B. _____

C. _____

D. _____

E. _____

F. _____

3. From the article "**Making Teamwork Work**," list and briefly describe the four ways to energize employees presented by the author.

A. _____

B. _____

C. _____

D. _____

4. Based on what you read in these two articles, discuss how you can follow the guidelines presented in "**Making Teamwork Work**" while avoiding the conditions presented in "**What You Can Learn**" in order to have a successful group.

_____

_____

_____

CHAPTER 18: Invitational Speaking

Activity 18.1: Handling Difficult Audience Members Invitationally

Summary of Activity: You will locate and read an article that presents advice about how to handle difficult participants in a classroom or other training situation. You will then consider the most and least helpful advice presented.

1. Locate and read "**t&d.com**" by **Ryan K. Ellis** (*hint: use "handling hecklers" as your textword search term in **PowerTrac**).

2. What are the two least helpful pieces of advice offered and why do you think they are unhelpful?

   _____

   _____

3. What are the two most helpful pieces of advice offered and why do you think they are helpful?

   _____

   _____

4. What is one way you might incorporate one of the helpful pieces of advice into the next speech you present where you encounter a hostile or difficult audience member?

   _____

   _____

5. What, in your opinion, are two primary motivations for an audience member to become hostile? Describe two things a hostile audience member might do that would really "push your buttons" that you would have trouble responding to invitationally. Role-playing with a classmate, come up with a strategy for responding invitationally to this kind of situation and then implement your strategy.

   _____

   _____

   _____

Activity 18.2: Understanding Conditions of Equality, Value and Self-Determination

Summary of Activity: You will locate and read an article about creating learning experiences. You will identify examples in the text of the article that illustrate the various conditions necessary to create an invitational environment.

1. Locate and read "**Train the Trainer: Trainers Need More Than Technical Talent or a Head for Business—They Need to Know How to Create Learning Experiences That Engage and Excite. Ensure Your Trainers Are Armed with the Teaching Tools to Do the Job Right**" by Suzette Hill (*hint: use "Train the Trainer" as your keyword search expression*).

2. Consider that in order to create an invitational environment, it is important that you create the three conditions of equality, value and self-determination. Read through the article and identify at least one example that helps create the condition of:

    A. Equality _____

    _____

    B. Value _____

    _____

    C. Self-Determination _____

    _____

3. Scan the article to approximately the third page until you find the statement "Adult learners share these characteristics." Read these 6 characteristics and describe how you can use this knowledge when delivering your own invitational speech.

    _____

    _____

    _____

4. Scan the article until you find the "10 Rules to Teach By." Choose two and describe how they might help you in preparing for your own invitational speech.

    _____

    _____

Activity 18.3: Understanding Innovative Leadership to Institute Change

Summary of Activity: You will locate and read an article that discusses the importance of adaptive leadership in today's society. You will consider different claims made in the article and address their relevance to Invitational Speaking.

1. Locate and read the article "**21st Century Pioneers: A New Kind of Leadership Must Emerge Across Our Public Schools to Ensure the Timely and Productive Adaptation of Our Institutions to Change**" by **Patricia Clark White** (*hint: use "respecting diversity" as your textword search expression in PowerTrac*).

2. Scan the article and locate the headings "Purpose and Vision" and "Creativity and Innovation." In your mind, how do the claims made in these paragraphs relate to the importance of the concept of Invitational Speaking?

   _____

   _____

   _____

3. Scan the article until you find the heading "Power and Authority," paying particular attention to the paragraph that begins, "Visionary leaders know that sharing power builds motivation . . . ." Why is this a particularly important concept to understand when preparing and delivering an invitational speech?

   _____

   _____

   _____

Activity 18.4: Defining and Addressing the Concept of Dialogue

Summary of Activity: You will locate, copy and read an article that provides different definitions of dialogue and its emerging importance in today's information age.

1. Locate and print **"Dialogue and Transformation" by Nancy C. Roberts** (*hint: use "Public Conversations Project" as your textword search term in PowerTrac*). NOTE: You do not have to read the entire article, you will simply need to read the first three paragraphs and scan the rest of it.

2. Read the first three paragraphs and describe your thoughts about the claim Roberts makes about transformational change and ways to encourage successful change. How, in your mind, is this related to what you are learning about invitational speaking?

    _____

    _____

    _____

3. Scan the article for the five definitions of dialogue (offered by Bohm; Linder; Gergen, McNamee, and Barrett; Isaac; and Bradley) and summarize these definitions in your own words here.

    _____

    _____

    _____

4. Scan to approximately the fifth page and read the paragraph that begins, "Unfortunately...Dewey believed there was a loss of dialogue...." How has dialogue in your own life been reduced by these factors? Reflect on ways you might be able to increase dialogue in your personal life and discuss your conclusions with a small group in class.

    _____

    _____

    _____